THE HEART
of LOVE

THE HEART
of LOVE

OBEYING GOD'S TWO
GREAT COMMANDMENTS

TED RIVERA

Previously published as *Divine Direction*

ZONDERVAN

The Heart of Love
Copyright © 2013 by Ted Rivera

Previously published as *Divine Direction*

This title is also available as a Zondervan ebook. Visit www.zondervan.com/ebooks.

Requests for information should be addressed to:

Zondervan, Grand Rapids, Michigan 49530

Library of Congress Cataloging-in-Publication Data

Rivera, Ted.
    The Heart of Love : Obeying God's Two Great Commandments / Ted Rivera.
        pages cm
    ISBN 978-0-310-51482-4
    1. Christian life. 2. Love—Religious aspects—Christianity. I. Title.
BV4501.3.R585 2013
248.4—dc23   2013014762

Cover design: Michelle Lenger
Cover photography: iStockphoto
Interior design: Matthew Van Zomeren and Ben Fetterley

Printed in the United States of America

13 14 15 16 17 1 8 19 20 /OPM/ 17 16 15 14 13 12 11 10 9 8 7 6 5 4 3 2 1

To my children
May you always see God's two great
commandments as both a calling and a joy.

CONTENTS

INTRODUCTION

WHAT DOES GOD WANT FROM MY LIFE? There are hundreds of commandments in the Bible, along with so much wisdom, that it seems impossible to process all this information. Some of the guidance in Scripture applies to major matters (e.g., "You shall not murder," Exod 20:13) and some to comparatively minor ones ("A gossip betrays a confidence, but a trustworthy person keeps a secret," Prov 11:13). Because of this, it's not surprising that Christians sometimes struggle to understand how best to live their lives. There are 1,189 chapters in the Bible. How do we make sense of it all? What's most important? We look to the churches we are a part of, to our pastors, and to other Christians to help us process and distill all of this information, but even then it can be hard to know what's best.

Happily, as surprising as it may seem, it's not hard to know what's most pleasing to God and, as a result, how we should be living. Jesus clearly explained this for us. One day, an expert in the law came to Jesus in order to test him and asked, "Teacher, which is the greatest commandment in the Law?" (Matt 22:36). Now, this sounds like a bad idea, doesn't it? Does it seem wise to test Jesus? Jesus, the beloved Son of God? Jesus, who was God incarnate? But rather than rebuke the man, Jesus took time to answer his question and, in doing so, gave us the essential starting point we need as we seek to understand how best to live the Christian life: "Jesus replied: '"Love the Lord your God with all your heart and with all your soul and with all your mind." This is the first and greatest commandment. And the second is like it: "Love your neighbor as yourself." All the Law and the Prophets hang on these two commandments' " (Matt 22:37 – 40).

In these few words, Jesus provides us with the key insight we need into how to understand the whole of the Bible and, as a result, how we should live a life that will be pleasing to our God. He teaches us that "all the Law and the Prophets hang on these two commandments." In other words, everything we find in the whole of Scripture can be shown to relate to these two commandments, as if the whole of Scripture could be pictured as two great trees with many branches and many more glorious leaves.

This realization leads us toward something we may have never known before. It is possible to obtain clear, trustworthy, divine direction and to develop a true heart of love. We can know with confidence how to lead lives that are pleasing to God. Both tremendous freedom and peace of mind come from knowing that the choices we make as Christians can be tested and found to be wise, and that we can have filters for our day-to-day decision-making that are based on biblical truth.

Unfortunately, too many Christians live each day making decisions that are disconnected from the fountain of the wisdom of Scripture. Thus, our goal is to consider carefully the two great commandments that Jesus points us to, and in doing so, we can understand not simply how to make good choices in our lives but the best ones. And let's be honest — this may keep us from making *bad* choices as well. Two great commandments. The *greatest* of commandments. What can we learn?

As we plunge into this study, let me set before you a challenge that will underscore for us the seriousness of what it is that we are about to undertake. You may have heard how the obituaries of famous people are sometimes written years before their death. In this way, as soon as they die, they can be mildly edited and published. This may seem a bit grim. But think about obituaries and the kind of information they contain. They typically report such matters as whom the deceased was related to, where he attended school, what she did for a living, and what he was most interested in. Every day, you and I are, in effect, writing our own obituaries. Are you satisfied with what you have accomplished in this life thus far?

But let's not stop there. We might be too quick to congratulate ourselves on our own accomplishments. As we consider our lives, we must strive to come to the end with as few regrets as possible. Can you imagine someone coming to the end of his life and saying, "Oh, if only I had watched more television!" Or, "Oh, if only I had mastered one more video game!" Or, "Oh, my life would have really mattered to others if I had been able to attend just one more sporting event!" But if our obituaries really expressed what was most often in our hearts, perhaps some of these things, or others like them, would appear.

Loving God and loving other people: now *that* seems like a life worth living. But this will only happen by deliberate action on our part. Our lives will ultimately be a success or a failure based on the choices we make every day. A couple of years ago, I lost ninety pounds. I can tell you that I had to make thousands of choices through the year it took me to lose that weight, and in the years that followed, thousands more choices to keep it off. Spiritually speaking, we could likely use a diet even more; I'd rather be the fattest person in heaven than the fittest person in hell. And so the seriousness of this task is now in view, and as the poet put it, "Only one life, 'twill soon be past, Only what's done for Christ will last."

chapter 1

LOVE *for* GOD

TAKE A MOMENT AND THINK about the most glorious wedding you have ever attended. It may have been your own wedding or the wedding of a friend or loved one; it may have taken place near your home or in a far-off place. But for a moment, allow your mind to wander back to that event. There may have been flowers and music; the bride and groom may have been bedecked in spectacular array. In some cultures, perhaps a horse-drawn carriage or expensive limousine transported the happy couple after the ceremony. Maybe the sun was shining. On that most perfect day, love was surely in the air. But add to this one other thought: Is a *marriage* the same thing as a *wedding*? Hardly! There are dirty dishes, and poopy diapers, and even arguments over things that ultimately are of little or no consequence.

The word *love* has been watered down in our day. Happily, the Bible removes any mystery about the real meaning of this term and helps us soberly understand what love for God looks like. Jesus said plainly, "If you love me, you will keep my commandments" (John 14:15 ESV). By doing what God wants, we demonstrate our love to him — not "with words or speech but with actions and in truth" (1 John 3:18).

In the gospel of Luke, Jesus paints a picture of what it is that a disciple will look like. It is a picture that serves as an excellent starting point, but also a terrific warning. If we're being honest with ourselves and with one another, at many points we may well be tempted to turn back. A disciple is ultimately a humble follower, someone who wants God's will to be done on earth in the same way it is done in heaven. And Jesus set this terrific test before us, to help us determine if we are on the right path: "If anyone comes to me and does not hate father and mother, wife and children, brothers and sisters — yes, even their own life — such a person cannot be my disciple. And whoever does not carry their cross and follow me cannot be my disciple" (Luke 14:26 – 27). In this short passage, we learn three potent truths.

THREE POTENT TRUTHS

1. Love for God Trumps Every Human Relationship

It is certainly the case that, throughout Scripture, we are told to love our families. The apostle Paul goes so far as to state: "Anyone who does not provide for their relatives, and especially for their own household, has denied the faith and is worse than an unbeliever" (1 Tim 5:8). But by comparison to our love for God, the love we should have for even our own families should be a distant second place.

Some struggle with this notion, but it's not hard to understand. Ultimately, we will all be better sons and daughters, better husbands and wives, and better children and friends if we love God supremely, above all other competitors. All of our decisions will ultimately most benefit our loved ones when we seek to glorify God as our chief and highest end.

2. Love for God Trumps My Own Life

Jesus here teaches us that we must love him more than we love ourselves. Once again, he points out that — by comparison to the love we have for God — we should hate ourselves! In an age when self-esteem is universally proclaimed as an essential human pursuit, this may well appear to us to be a particularly peculiar notion. But if we understand better who God is and consider his goodness, his glories, and his work among us, it is almost as if self-regard disappears. The man or woman who catches a clear sight of God will lose the self-obsession so common in our day.

In a little book written many years ago entitled *The Self Life and the Christ Life*, A. B. Simpson offered this compelling perspective: "We are to yield ourselves unto God as those who have already died and are alive from the dead, recognizing the cross as behind us; and for this very reason presenting ourselves to God, to be used for His service and glory."[1]

3. Love for God Will Result in Suffering

What sane person would choose suffering? Let's begin with this urgent observation: a willingness to suffer is not an option. Jesus says here that if we are unwilling to carry our cross, we *cannot be his disciple*. The cross is no mere ornament, no fashion statement; it was a place to die. In our day, carrying a cross would be the equivalent of traveling with one's personal electric chair or lethal injection kit: people died gruesome deaths on Roman crosses.

I am sure we have all heard tens of thousands of

commercials and seen tens of thousands of billboards aimed at selling us ever new ways to be more comfortable. Can you imagine, for example, a car commercial that said: "Get in! Our seats are painful!" But Jesus is no salesman. He promises that if we would be his disciples, our common, daily, and serious expectation is a future of suffering. He was our chief example in this, who "for the joy set before him endured the cross, scorning its shame, and sat down at the right hand of the throne of God. Consider him who endured such opposition from sinners, so that you will not grow weary and lose heart" (Heb 12:2b–3).

In this light, if we are being honest with ourselves and understand rightly the kind of love we are considering, we may very well want to turn back now. Sadly, many who call themselves Christians in our day will not meet the criteria represented by these three potent truths. Jesus warned his hearers, "Not everyone who says to me, 'Lord, Lord,' will enter the kingdom of heaven, but only the one who does the will of my Father who is in heaven" (Matt 7:21). But if in fact we want to express a genuine love for God, it is important that — as Jesus asserted — we count the cost. Are you still sure that you want to love God as Jesus directed?

THE FIRST AND GREATEST COMMANDMENT

As we have seen, Jesus taught us that the first and greatest commandment is, "Love the Lord your God with all your heart and with all your soul and with all your mind" (Matt 22:37). It's interesting to note that in the gospel of Mark, this statement of Jesus appears with slightly different wording. In Mark 12:30 we read, "Love the Lord your God with all your heart and with all your soul and with all your mind and with all your strength." Is this a discrepancy? Is this addition of the idea of *strength* important?

The most important thing to note here may instead be the intensity of this commandment, more so than the fact that *heart, mind, soul,* and *strength* are specifically mentioned. I think the paraphrase known as *The Message* gets the spirit of this statement right: "Love the Lord God with all your passion and prayer and intelligence and energy." We are really being taught here to love God with absolutely everything we have, with absolutely everything that we are. And this is no minor matter: it's the first and greatest commandment! The most important word in this commandment may be the little word "all." There must be no part of who we are that we are not willing to lay before God on the altar. In the same way that Abraham was willing to slay Isaac in obedience to the command of God, we must go one step further: we must be willing to slay even our own wants and desires, our self-interest, and our self-regard.

Here, then, is our starting point. We can begin by posing this question: "What does it mean to love God with everything I am?" It's also worth taking a moment to ask, "Is this even something I want?" It's one thing to be open to the idea of living our lives in a manner that will most please God. It's quite another thing to actually seek to do it, all the time, to the highest degree possible. But notice that what I *want* as a Christian is of secondary importance. This is, after all, a commandment and not a suggestion.

As such, I'm going to ask you to do something that you might not want to do at this particular moment. You are a busy person. You've somehow found time to read a book—I commend you! But now, I'm nevertheless going to ask you to pause for a moment and pray about this. You should ask God to show you your own heart. As I've sought to pray while writing, you should now ask him to show you your own heart and teach you how you might live out this commandment day to day.

It might be prudent for you to open your Bible to Matthew 22:37 or Mark 12:30 and pray over this first great commandment in the larger context of the passage where these texts appear. In the pages that follow, a few of the implications of this first great commandment will be presented. But an even better starting point will be for you to get on your knees—physically or metaphorically—and ask God to give you a heart that hungers for him, a mind keen to serve him, a desire to serve him with everything you are, so that you might above all things desire to be sold out to him, holding him first in your heart.

In the following pages, we will consider some of the primary ways in which we are called to love God: in worship, in our communion and baptism, in our private and corporate Bible study, in prayer, and in our giving. There are, of course, many other ways by which our love to God can and must be expressed. That said, as we reflect on the command to love God with all our heart, soul, mind, and strength, we should not be surprised to see these elements appear. This is a starting point for us as we seek to unpack this first and greatest of all the commandments of God.

chapter 2

WORSHIP

IT IS COMMON IN OUR DAY to hear people say, "I can worship God anywhere. I don't need to be in a church to worship God." You might also hear statements such as, "I feel closest to God in nature, enjoying his creation." It's certainly true that God can be worshiped anywhere and that one can feel close to God by experiencing the splendor of creation. But ultimately, this is just not enough to satisfy our souls. More importantly — since we are considering what it means to love God aright — it is not enough to love God by ourselves, on our own. There is something profound — something wholly wonderful — that takes place in corporate worship. Evidently, our love for God is something that is best shared with others who love him too. It would seem in this light that the idea of somehow loving God on our own is an extreme form of selfishness!

We read about something of the urgency of this matter in the book of Hebrews: "And let us consider how we may spur one another on toward love and good deeds, not giving up meeting together, as some are in the habit of doing, but encouraging one another — and all the more as you see the Day approaching" (Heb 10:24-25).

We are here encouraged to "consider" this, how it is that we might "spur one another on toward love": love for God, evidently, and love for our fellow human beings (i.e., "good deeds"). We are actively, earnestly, and enthusiastically to encourage one another in this. It's hard to satisfy the aim of this commandment while worshiping God on our own under an evergreen tree. And more plainly, we see that it is wrong to give up "meeting together, as some are in the habit of doing."

Warnings are positive things. Now truthfully, when someone warns us, we do not always receive these warnings cheerfully. But we must be warned that the worship of God is not something that we can undertake casually, or occasionally, or halfheartedly. Jesus once warned the Pharisees, quoting the prophet Isaiah from of old, "These people honor me with their lips, but their hearts are far from me. They worship me in vain; their teachings are merely human rules" (Matt 15:8 – 9). It should set us trembling to consider that we might think we are worshiping God in a manner that pleases him, but ultimately find out that the opposite was true. It is better to be warned about the seriousness of approaching God in the way he wants us to worship him than to find out too late that we missed the boat.

While we rightly recognize that, with the coming of the new covenant, a new and better path to worship is ours, it is healthy from time to time to consider the *old* covenant, the *old* way of worship. Go through the first five books of the Bible with this aim in mind. Particularly in Exodus, Leviticus, Numbers, and Deuteronomy, you will find all kinds of offerings described and a manner of sacrifice that is, perhaps above all else, extraordinarily precise. If you consider the commandments that governed this worship as a whole, you will quickly understand that God himself set before his people an incredibly precise and demanding set of laws that were to be followed to the letter. Uzzah died when he steadied the ark while it was being transported (see 2 Sam 6). The Sabbath was reserved as a day devoted and consecrated to God. How serious were these laws? Many of them were literally matters of life and death to the people of Israel. As one of many possible examples, consider Numbers 15:32–36:

> While the Israelites were in the wilderness, a man was found gathering wood on the Sabbath day. Those who found him gathering wood brought him to Moses and Aaron and the whole assembly, and they kept him in custody, because it was not clear what should be done to him. Then the LORD said to Moses, "The man must die. The whole assembly must stone him outside the camp." So the assembly took him outside the camp and stoned him to death, as the LORD commanded Moses.

Happily, we no longer live under these strictures in the era of the new covenant that Christ has ushered in. But notice that these laws were not the invention of human beings. You see here in Numbers 15 that it is God himself who decreed that the man who violated the Sabbath simply by gathering wood had committed a sin so grievous as to warrant death. We might think to ourselves, "That's not fair!" Instead, we should put our hands to our mouths for a moment and reflect, asking, "If worship was so important under the old covenant, how much more important it is now that we have come to understand God so much more fully!"

Imagine for a moment that you find yourself in a church service you find boring. It happens. Certainly, it could be a problem with the church you are attending or in one you are perhaps visiting. But the problem could also lie elsewhere: within us. Clearly, the *object* of our affection is not flawed in any way. The purpose of worship is, after all, not entertainment; instead, the goal of worship is the glory of God. David, referred to in Scripture as a man after God's own heart (Acts 13:22), proclaimed:

> I will extol the LORD at all times;
> his praise will always be on my lips.
> I will glory in the LORD;
> let the afflicted hear and rejoice.
> Glorify the LORD with me;
> let us exalt his name together. (Ps 34:1 – 3)

We sometimes chide children for fidgeting in church services, but we are wise to correct our own fickle hearts as well. In both Isaiah and Revelation, we see our God described as "holy, holy, holy" (Isa 6:3; Rev 4:8). The Lord is perfect in every way and infinitely worthy of our worship. Thus, if, while we seek to worship him, there is imperfection in either our church or in us, this does not diminish God's goodness in the least. In such circumstances, what would constitute worship that is most pleasing to God?

WORSHIP THAT IS PLEASING TO GOD BEGINS WITH THE WORD OF GOD

If you talk to people about how they went about choosing the church they are a part of, you will get a wide range of possible answers. You might hear, "I *loved* the praise band!" or, "I was greeted warmly when I first attended," or, "The youth group had children in it near the age of my own children," or even, "The potluck suppers are amazing!" But if we are trying to identify a church that worships God in a manner that is most pleasing to him, it makes sense for us to begin with this premise: the Word of God must be the nonnegotiable centerpiece of worship.

Theologians refer to the Bible as *special revelation*. This means simply that we recognize the Bible and, in particular, the preaching of the Word as an even more profound means of communication from God to us than either creation or our conscience. Creation and our consciences can give us *general* revelation about God; we see, for example, in creation that he is powerful, wise, and even artistic. Many people obtain from their conscience a general sense of right or wrong. But in the Word of God, we come to know him specifically. In this way, we learn not only about him in a general way, but we learn about what pleases him and how to approach him.

In writing to his protégé Timothy, the apostle Paul urged, "Until I come, devote yourself to the public reading of Scripture, to preaching and to teaching" (1 Tim 4:13). This advice still applies today. In our churches, in our services of worship, the public reading, preaching, and teaching of the Word of God remain our essential starting point. Our music, our announcements, our prayers, our giving — everything must be imbued with the Scriptures, and the churches we are a part of should make every effort to esteem the Word of God highly.

In worship, then, we seek to return to God something that he is due. We are seeking to "ascribe to the LORD the glory due his name" (1 Chr 16:29a). And Jesus taught us, "God is spirit, and his worshipers must worship in the Spirit and in truth" (John 4:24). And as we participate, we must be constantly weighing what we hear against the Word. If those who lived in Berea in ancient times were comparing what the apostle Paul said against Scripture (cf. Acts 17:10 – 11), how much more should we?

WORSHIP THAT IS PLEASING TO GOD ESTEEMS JESUS

Consider the prologue to John's gospel: "In the beginning was the Word, and the Word was with God, and the Word was God.... The Word became flesh and made his dwelling among us. We have seen his glory, the glory of the one and only Son, who came from the Father, full of grace and truth" (John 1:1, 14). Certainly, we learn here that Jesus is God and that Jesus became a man, living among us. But does this not also give us insight into how intimately connected our God is to his Word? His own Son, our Lord Jesus, is spoken of as "the Word," the divine Word. Is it not the case that all of Scripture reveals something about who God is and that the culmination of Scripture is the revelation of Jesus, his Son? As we begin our worship by featuring the Word of God, then, we should not be surprised that it leads us to God's own beloved Son: "This is my Son, whom I love; with him I am well pleased" (Matt 3:17b).

Throughout the whole of the Old Testament, the coming Messiah is in view. Throughout the whole of the New Testament, Jesus is set before us as the one through whom we come to the Father. Paul's statements in Philippians 2 represent one of hundreds of passages where Jesus is set before our eyes as our example, as our Savior:

> Who, being in very nature God,
> > did not consider equality with God something to
> > > be used to his own advantage;
> rather, he made himself nothing
> > by taking the very nature of a servant,
> > being made in human likeness.
> And being found in appearance as a man,
> > he humbled himself
> > by becoming obedient to death —
> > > even death on a cross!

Therefore God exalted him to the highest place
    and gave him the name that is above every
        name,
that at the name of Jesus every knee should bow,
    in heaven and on earth and under the earth,
and every tongue acknowledge that Jesus Christ is
        Lord,
    to the glory of God the Father. (Phil 2:6 – 11)

Every knee is to "bow" before him. This is a clarion call to worship our God in Jesus Christ.

WORSHIP IS NOT ABOUT US

Many churches today are focused on ensuring that visitors are warmly greeted, that the music is contemporary, and that those who attend feel comfortable. Sermons, some would suggest, must be entertaining and, above all, brief. All of these factors, though, focus on us: our needs, our interests, our desires. But if our aim is to love God, consider how different the attitude must be that we should bring to worship. The concern is not "What can I get out of this?" so much as "What can I put into this?" Paul warned, "For the time will come when people will not put up with sound doctrine. Instead, to suit their own desires, they will gather around them a great number of teachers to say what their itching ears want to hear" (2 Tim 4:3).

Think about this a bit differently. Most people like chocolate. It's hard to imagine a chocolate lover saying, "I just want a little bit." No! "Give me more!" would be their mantra. If we claim to love God, would we ever want to check our watch to see if the service was going to end on time? Wouldn't we instead be the one secretly hoping, "Oh, give me more of Christ!" This attitude, it seems, conveys something of the psalmist's heart, as we read:

> As the deer pants for streams of water,
>> so my soul pants for you, my God.
> My soul thirsts for God, for the living God.
>> When can I go and meet with God? (Ps 42:1 – 2)

Once again, it might well be wise to pause and pray. In this case, it would be good for us to examine carefully our own attitudes as we think about participating in worship. Here are just a few of the possible questions we might consider:

- What is my attitude toward corporate worship? Do I view it purely as a duty, or is it also a joy? Do I seek out worship even while traveling on vacation, or do I think that I somehow would benefit from a break?
- Do I pray in advance about worship services I attend? Am I concerned that God would be glorified in these services? Is there anything that I do in order to help ensure the success of a given worship service?
- Do I pray for those who lead? Do I pray for those who participate, as well as my own heart?
- Do I prepare for worship? Do I get adequate rest in advance? Do I bring my Bible and perhaps a notebook?
- Is my manner of dress (whether simple or formal) somehow a potential distraction to others in some way, or has my aim been to glorify God in this aspect of my preparation?
- Do I seek out others who might worship along with me? Do I pray for those who might come with me?
- Do I plan to arrive with plenty of time? Do I prepare my heart as we enter worship?

- Do I prepare to give more than just my money to God? Is worship somehow a key feature of my week?

While in worship itself, there may be a great many other possible questions to consider:

- Am I listening? Am I paying close attention? Am I nodding off?
- Am I singing along (regardless of my skill level)?
- Am I giving? Am I giving with a cheerful heart?
- Am I serving others in some way, if needed?
- Am I heeding the Word I hear?

We often speak of our time of worship as a worship *service*. This is precisely how we should view these times together: as a corporate opportunity to focus not on ourselves but on serving our Lord by means of our worship. The psalmist declared, "Great is the LORD and most worthy of praise; his greatness no one can fathom" (Ps 145:3). Worship is the very business of heaven itself, the chief preoccupation of the saints of God: "In a loud voice they were saying: 'Worthy is the Lamb, who was slain, to receive power and wealth and wisdom and strength and honor and glory and praise!' " (Rev 5:12).

WORSHIP IS INDEED WONDERFUL

A. W. Tozer wrote, "To meditate on the three Persons of the Godhead is to walk in thought through the garden eastward in Eden and to tread on holy ground. Our sincerest effort to grasp the incomprehensible mystery of the Trinity must remain forever futile, and only by deepest reverence can it be saved from actual presumption."[1] Tozer is echoing here on earth what we will know most fully in heaven: that God is splendid beyond all words, and our most heroic efforts will fall short of the glory due his name. We have seen that, day and night, worship never ceases in heaven (Rev 4:8). The angels themselves declare antiphonally again and again the wonders of our God.

If you have never caught sight of the sacred in this lifetime, you will content yourself with cheap descriptions of heaven as a place where people shop, or play golf, or drink beer with abandon. By contrast, all who have been born again (cf. John 3:3) have, on at least one occasion in life, seen God for who he is; they have caught sight of something of his magnificence. To see God in this way is not something one could ever tire of, but instead is something one can never again live without. If worship does not appear wonderful to you, you are right to ask God, "Have I been born again, born from above?" As the Scripture declares, "Everyone who calls on the name of the Lord will be saved" (Rom 10:13). Only then will you too find worship a wonder beyond all words. Again, Tozer offers us fit counsel here:

> A survey of church history will prove that it was those who were the yearning worshipers who also became the great workers. Those great saints whose hymns we so tenderly sing were active in their faith to the point that we must wonder how they ever did it all.
>
> The great hospitals have grown out of the hearts of worshiping men. The mental institutions grew out of the hearts of worshiping and compassionate men and women. We should say, too, that wherever the church has come out of her lethargy, rising from her sleep and into the tides of revival and spiritual renewal, always the worshipers were back of it.

We will be making a mistake if we just stand back and say, "But if we give ourselves to worship, no one will do anything."

On the contrary, if we give ourselves to God's call to worship, everyone will do more than he or she is doing now. Only, what he or she does will have significance and meaning to it. It will have the quality of eternity in it — it will be gold, silver and precious stones, not wood, hay and stubble.[2]

Do you find worship wonderful or mundane? How can we strive to make it ever more wonderful in our own eyes and in the eyes of our churches? I pray that together we can speak of worship and sing of worship such that we can testify, along with John Peterson's great hymn, that "heaven came down, and glory filled my soul."

chapter 3

COMMUNION
and BAPTISM

REMEMBER: everything we're considering in this first section relates to our love for God in some important way, and baptism and communion are no exceptions. Baptism and communion were both instituted by God and are public in nature; they are each a living sermon, since both baptism and communion are a public display of our personal and corporate love for and faith in God. Baptism is a form of public testimony, a declaration of one's wholehearted identification with Christ. The very idea of being baptized *in a secret manner* goes against the intent of the act. Similarly, there is no such thing as *individual* communion; the very word points us toward our *common union* in Christ. If our aim is to love God, both of these signs, both of these sacraments and seals, are not mere options but essentials.

BAPTISM

I can remember spending an evening several years ago in the apartment of a poor family in the city of Iași on the eastern border of Romania. This was at a point in time shortly after the fall of hard-line communism in that country, and along with a few others, I was able to travel through the country teaching and preaching in various settings. Until we arrived that night, the family had been sitting in the dark rather than use their electricity. We were served a simple meal that represented the best this family could afford.

This family had suffered greatly under the communist regime; in particular, the daughter had risked her life at one time in order to be baptized. Her family had been interrogated shortly afterward, but, inexplicably, no immediate harm came to them. They told us, though, of others who had not been so fortunate. This young woman's baptism had to be done in public. She was testifying to the world of her identification with Christ. By contrast, some I have known elsewhere have put off the command to be baptized because they "don't like water" or for some other similarly superficial reason. Can we really pretend to love God if we intentionally ignore the most basic commandments? By the world's standards, this family in Iaşi was poor, but they were filled with a joy I have rarely seen in others.

Let's first consider some of the basic truths associated with baptism. In the same way that the doctrine of justification signifies our initial spiritual acceptance by God through faith in Jesus Christ, baptism signifies this same truth in a visible, physical way as we enter the waters. Consider the following principles that help us flesh out something of its significance.

Baptism is an initiation rite. True, it is not mandatory that someone be baptized in order to be saved. Take the case of the thief on the cross, who we are told is in paradise, but he was never baptized (Luke

23:39 – 43). Nevertheless, the expectation is that the connection between faith and baptism is — or should be — nearly immediate. In the Great Commission, which we will consider later, we are commanded to "go and make disciples of all nations, *baptizing them ...* " (Matt 28:19 – 20). After Peter's sermon on Pentecost, he proclaimed, "Repent and be baptized," and those who repented were baptized immediately (Acts 2:38 – 41). Thus, baptism is commanded and should be undertaken early in one's Christian walk as a humble act of obedience.

Baptism communicates our identification with Jesus Christ. The apostle Paul writes, "We were therefore buried with him through baptism into death in order that, just as Christ was raised from the dead through the glory of the Father, we too may live a new life" (Rom 6:4). As we enter the waters of baptism, we identify with Jesus' death, burial, and resurrection. Although 1 Corinthians 6 is talking about avoiding sexual immorality, Paul's statement there seems equally applicable to baptism: "You were bought at a price. Therefore honor God with your bodies" (1 Cor 6:20).

Baptism also represents our cleansing from sin and our indwelling by the Holy Spirit. John the Baptist is featured throughout the Gospels preaching a gospel of repentance, standing in the waters of the Jordan and calling for his hearers to enter. He proclaimed, "I baptize you with water for repentance. But after me comes one who is more powerful than I, whose sandals I am not worthy to carry. He will baptize you with the Holy Spirit and with fire" (Matt 3:11). In the same way that water cleanses physically, the waters of baptism communicate something of the spiritual cleansing that is ours in Christ. We read, "He saved us, not because of righteous things we had done, but because of his mercy. He saved us through the washing of rebirth and renewal by the Holy Spirit" (Titus 3:5). In the same way that Naaman the leper entered the waters of the Jordan River and was cleansed (cf. 2 Kgs 5), we also proclaim how we ourselves have been cleansed by the washing of rebirth, which is made public by means of our baptism.

Baptism is a testimony, a proclamation of our faith, love, and obedience. Why else would we do this? Baptism is not a typical human act; rather, it is a public demonstration of what God has done in our hearts and lives. Once we have trusted Christ as Savior, it is a healthy sign that we desire to share with others what has taken place. Baptism offers such an opportunity. While baptism conducted in a church building can certainly provide a public venue for this testimony, there is something to be said for finding ways to get outside where all the world can see.

In my closet upstairs are several shirts that bear the emblem of the Chicago Cubs. When I was a child, no one told me that the Cubs were not noted for their winning ways. Despite this, I have socks with their logo on them, a couple of jackets, and trinkets too numerous to count. By these things I testify to my connection with this team. Of far greater import, baptism is the Christian's way to identify with and herald that which she holds most dear.

We naturally tell others about many things we identify with; by being baptized, we have occasion to declare, "I love God, and I'm not ashamed to admit it." It is also important to recognize that, since God commanded us to be baptized, we should not be surprised that he is often present in a unique way on these occasions. Often, baptism is accompanied by the testimony of the one who is baptized; it's almost as if we just can't help proclaim,

"I will not die but live, and will proclaim what the LORD has done" (Ps 118:17).

COMMUNION

In the church of which my family is a part, it is customary for a number of us, from time to time, to bring communion to members who are no longer physically able to be present with us. In a real way, we are able to convey to them that they are still a part of us, that together we share a common bond. But what is this bond about? It's not chiefly about us. Yes, certainly we are conveying something of the connection we have with one another. But, supremely, this is an occasion once again that begins with love for our God in Christ.

In the same way that the doctrine of sanctification signifies our ongoing relationship with and growth in God, so also communion, in regularly taking the bread and wine, signifies our dependence on and relationship to God. The starting point for any explanation of communion is the idea of remembrance. Each time we observe the Lord's Supper, we are saying corporately, "We remember your tremendous sacrifice, Lord Jesus — your suffering, your death, on behalf of us as sinners." Jesus himself taught us to "do this in remembrance of me" (Luke 22:19b). In other words, communion is another kind of sermon, as we "proclaim the Lord's death until he comes" (1 Cor 11:26b).

In the bread, we are to see, as it were, the broken body of our Lord. In the wine, we are to see his blood, poured out to satisfy the wrath of God against our sins. The one who takes the elements of bread and wine and fails to discern the Lord's body "eats and drinks judgment" on himself or herself (1 Cor 11:29). This is an extraordinarily urgent matter. Paul warns, "That is why many among you are weak and sick, and a number of you have fallen asleep" (1 Cor 11:30). Note that Paul is talking here about *permanent* sleep, the sleep of death!

How intimate is our relationship with God supposed to be? The intimacy of the union with Christ that is to be ours is illustrated by the potent imagery that serves as the basis for the Lord's Supper. Jesus said, "Whoever eats my flesh and drinks my blood remains in me, and I in him" (John 6:56). When Jesus said this, the Jews who heard him were shocked by this imagery. Clearly, Jesus conveys by the symbols of the bread (as his flesh) and the wine (as his blood) that we remain in Christ, and he remains in us: "Christ in you, the hope of glory" (Col 1:27b). If we long for intimacy with Christ, we should anticipate and prepare for the Lord's Table.

Our dependence on God is also typified by communion. The common elements of bread and wine are seen as life-giving and nourishing. Jesus uses the image of a vine, which underscores our dependence on and connection to him: "I am the vine; you are the branches. If you remain in me and I in you, you will bear much fruit; apart from me you can do nothing" (John 15:5). How long do we think we would survive without our God? Paul writes, "In him [Christ] all things hold together" (Col 1:17b). I am reminded of the image used by the prophet Zechariah. The Messiah — the coming Lord Jesus — is spoken of as the "tent peg" (Zech 10:4). Like other divinely inspired writers, Peter refers to him as the "cornerstone" (e.g., 1 Pet 2:6–7). For us as believers, Jesus holds it all together. In our time of communion with him and with one another, we testify to this.

Finally, communion provides us with a regular opportunity to evaluate our relationship with God:

"Everyone ought to examine themselves before they eat of the bread and drink of the cup" (1 Cor 11:28). All of us sin. The purpose of this self-examination is not intended to help us determine whether we have earned the right to participate in communion because we have been particularly obedient of late. Instead, as we examine ourselves — and see our sins, our failings, and our short-comings all too easily — we are compelled to *remember* our great, cavernous need for Jesus. So also we are compelled to remember the Bible's call to holiness and obedience, the fruit of a life of love.

I once confessed to a man something I did not think was controversial. I said, echoing the words of many others throughout church history, "I am a sinner saved by grace." I didn't even go so far as John Newton in his hymn "Amazing Grace," who testified that God has saved a "wretch like me." I was simply trying to explain to this man how grateful I was to God for his saving work and to acknowledge openly and honestly that, even as a Christian, I feel keenly the need for salvation. This man shocked me with his passionate response: "Speak for yourself."

It's important for us to recognize every time we take communion together that we are declaring to our Lord and to one another that, indeed, we are sinners saved by grace. Even the apostle John, known throughout history as the beloved disciple, wrote, "If we claim to be without sin, we deceive ourselves and the truth is not in us" (1 John 1:8). Whenever we remember Jesus and his titanic sacrifice on our behalf, we cannot help but examine ourselves and be reminded of how great our need was for that saving work. This surely brings forth love toward God in the believer's heart!

chapter 4

CORPORATE
and PRIVATE
BIBLE STUDY

WHEN WE INITIALLY BECOME CHRISTIANS, the first advice given to us is usually this: "Be sure to read your Bible!" It's good advice, but unfortunately there are two stories I can share, both of which took place at graduate seminaries, that illustrate how great a challenge this can be. It's worth emphasizing for the moment that seminaries, of course, are where pastors and other spiritual leaders go for training.

The first story comes from a large class of perhaps three hundred students attending an introductory class on the Old Testament. The professor asked one simple question: "How many of you have read the whole of the Old Testament?" Bear in mind that this is a committed group of people! Most had decided not only to follow Christ, but to serve him in their life's work. Despite this, no more than *half* of the hands of those students went up — and one has to imagine that more than a few students raised their hands only because they were too embarrassed to acknowledge in this public way that they themselves had not yet read the entire Old Testament.

The second story is similar and comes from a different seminary. Once again, the class size was large. The question put to this group was similar to that of the first: "How many of you read your Bibles for thirty minutes each day?" In this case, the proportion of students who were able to raise their hands was small indeed.

It can be encouraging to us to hear that even seminary students can struggle to be as consistent or as successful in reading and studying their Bibles as they should be. But let's remember what our goal is: we want to live a life full of love for God, recognizing this as the first and greatest of all commandments. If, then, the Bible is the source of special revelation that God has set in place to convey truth to us about every circumstance of life, shouldn't it be a tremendous priority for us, both as individuals and in our churches?

PERSONAL BIBLE STUDY

Hundreds of plans have been devised to read and study the Bible systematically. My personal favorite was created by Robert Murray M'Cheyne; his plan has served our family well.* But the simple truth is, there are five basic rules that will help you profit most from your Bible reading:

1. *Don't just start reading at Genesis and make your way forward.* It's better to use an approach that has you reading a bit from the New Testament and a bit from the Old. Can you read the Bible from start to finish? Yes,

---

* For one example of this plan, see http://hippocampus extensions.com/mcheyneplan/ (accessed March 27, 2013).

certainly. I'm simply suggesting that this approach may prove more challenging than necessary. The aim is to benefit as much as possible from your reading. You will certainly find some biblical books more difficult than others. Using a plan that selects from different parts of the Bible each day will help you avoid getting bogged down and discouraged.

2. *Read consistently.* While the seminary students in the second example above weren't as successful as their professor may have liked, the key really is to be as consistent as possible. It certainly should be our goal to read the whole Bible. Is there anything God has said that we shouldn't be interested in? Find a time of day that works best for you and stick with it. After all, the goal is not to read the Bible through once completely and say to ourselves, "Phew! Glad that's done!" On the contrary, reading the Bible must become for us a lifelong habit, a means by which we are able to draw near to God by his Word and receive the promptings of his Holy Spirit as we meditate and prayerfully reflect.

3. *Remember to pray.* It's astonishing how many people will say things like this: "I try to read the Bible, but I have trouble understanding it." Now surely, it may be that the portion of the Bible they are reading is particularly challenging (in which case, a good study Bible may be of help, as well as other good resources). But it's amazing how rarely Christians realize that a part of why they are having trouble understanding the Bible may simply be that they have failed to recognize that it is a *spiritual* book! The psalmist prayed, "Open my eyes that

I may see wonderful things in your law" (Ps 119:18), and this simple prayer would serve us well as we approach our time in the Word. We may be able to download the Bible just like any other book and start reading it on our favorite electronic device, but it is not just any book. These are the very words of God. We must cry out to him and seek to understand each and every phrase we come across.

4. *If you are having trouble understanding something, you might take a few extra minutes later in your day to look up the word or concept that seemed foreign.* I find it interesting that we chide teenagers for a lack of diligence if they fail to pick up subjects such as calculus or physics, but we ourselves give up when there is the slightest challenge before us as we open our Bibles. We too need to learn to work hard, as the benefits are incalculably profound. Paul wrote to Timothy, "Do your best to present yourself to God as one approved, a worker who does not need to be ashamed and who correctly handles the word of truth" (2 Tim 2:15). Jesus warned a prospective disciple one day, "No one who puts his hand to the plow and looks back is fit for service in the kingdom of God" (Luke 9:62).

5. *Seek to apply what you are reading to your life.* Each day, as you consider a portion of Scripture, pray that God will show you how you should be living out the truths you are considering. As James counsels,

Do not merely listen to the word, and so deceive yourselves. Do what it says. Anyone who listens to

the word but does not do what it says is like someone who looks at his face in a mirror and, after looking at himself, goes away and immediately forgets
what he looks like. But whoever looks intently into
the perfect law that gives freedom, and continues
in it — not forgetting what they have heard, but
doing it — they will be blessed in what they do. (Jas
1:22–25)

Have you ever had a challenging coworker or a discouraged (or discouraging) family member? Have you
ever faced struggles and trials? It seems impossible to
get through a single day, and at times a single hour,
without trials of some kind! The Word of God gives for
every circumstance of life "apples of gold in settings of
silver" (Prov 25:11). In many ways, it is utterly amazing
that we have to encourage one another to read and study
Scripture; the benefits should be so obvious, and chief
among these benefits is nearness to God himself. Jer-
emiah exclaimed, "When your words came, I ate them;
they were my joy and my heart's delight, for I bear your
name, LORD God Almighty" (Jer 15:16). Job, who knew
suffering like few others, went so far as to say, "I have
not departed from the commands of his lips; I have
treasured the words of his mouth more than my daily
bread" (Job 23:12). Do we prize God's Word even more
than food?

CORPORATE BIBLE STUDY

There are at least two basic ways that Bible study is typically done in our churches: in Sunday school programs
(before or after worship) and in small group Bible stud-
ies that take place during the week. You should view
such options as a vital complement to your individual

Bible study. In such groups, you will often be able to ask questions or participate in discussions, which will help your understanding deepen. You will also be able to bless others with your own insights. Consider this counsel from the book of Ecclesiastes:

> Two are better than one,
>> because they have a good return for their labor:
> If either of them falls down,
>> one can help the other up.
> But pity anyone who falls
>> and has no one to help them up!
> Also, if two lie down together, they will keep warm.
>> But how can one keep warm alone?
> Though one may be overpowered,
>> two can defend themselves.
> A cord of three strands is not quickly broken.
>> (Eccl 4:9 – 12)

Perhaps your church doesn't have a Bible study. Why not start one? Begin with one or two members of your congregation, and urge along a family member or two. Before you know it, you have a small group Bible study emerging. Don't think you're fit to lead one? Neither did Moses. Do it anyway. We read:

> Moses said to the LORD, "Pardon your servant, Lord. I have never been eloquent, neither in the past nor since you have spoken to your servant. I am slow of speech and tongue."
>
> The LORD said to him, "Who gave human beings their mouths? Who makes them deaf or mute? Who gives them sight or makes him blind? Is it not I, the LORD? Now go; I will help you speak and will teach you what to say." (Ex 4:10 – 12)

chapter 5

THE LIFE *of* PRAYER

THE GOSPEL OF LUKE provides an interesting window into the life of Jesus. Note his teaching about prayer: "He said to them, 'When you pray, say: "Father, hallowed be your name, your kingdom come. Give us each day our daily bread. Forgive us our sins, for we also forgive everyone who sins against us. And lead us not into temptation"'" (Luke 11:2–4).* It's important to note, though, that Jesus wasn't just *teaching* about prayer on this occasion, but he was also *praying* (11:1); this is apparently what prompted a question from the disciples about prayer.

Earlier in Luke's gospel, we gain an important insight along these lines. Luke writes, "Jesus often withdrew to lonely places and prayed" (Luke 5:16). It's important for us to reflect on why this might be the case. Did Jesus do this in order to set an example for the disciples to follow? This doesn't seem to be the most important reason

---

* It's apparently the case that Jesus taught the disciples to pray on more than one occasion. In Matthew 6, this same prayer appears with slightly different words, and the occasion is different: it appears in the midst of the Sermon on the Mount.

for Jesus' prayer; otherwise, why retreat to lonely places? Jesus, we are told, did this "often." Jesus felt the need to spend time alone with the Father. His relationship with the Father was intimate and permanent.

Near the time of his crucifixion, Jesus told the disciples, "A time is coming and in fact has come, when you will be scattered, each to your own home. You will leave me all alone. Yet I am not alone, for my Father is with me" (John 16:32). We find him in prayer at Gethsemane in the final moment of freedom he knew prior to his trial and crucifixion. His surely was a life filled with prayer. Even on the cross, we hear the plaintive cry, *"'Eli, Eli, lema sabachthani?'* (which means, 'My God, my God, why have you forsaken me?')" (Matt 27:46b).

As Christians, it's important for us to compare this attitude with our own attitude toward prayer. For Jesus, prayer appeared to be as essential to his spiritual life as oxygen is to our physical lives. In many churches, listen to the prayer requests that are lifted up. Perhaps 90 percent or more have to do with concerns for someone's health or well-being. By contrast, it appears as if Jesus spent time with the Father because he *loved* him. He *wanted* to be with him in these seasons of prayer. He went off on his own so that he could be alone with the Father. It was a fundamental, consistent priority in his life.

If the only times we pray are when we have need for health or healing, or when we need to express concern for a loved one, or when we half-mumble a mealtime prayer, we are missing out on the intimacy intended. In the Lord's Prayer, Jesus touched on several areas that should occupy our minds as we approach the Father.

We should praise God for who he is: "Hallowed be your name." This word, *hallowed*, is an ancient one. Few translations attempt to update this term. It conveys well the reverence, the awe, the holiness of God. We hear in this statement echoes of that era of Old Testament history when God's people did not even know his name. God had only revealed himself by the designation "I AM WHO I AM" (Ex 3:14). When we consider all the ways that God is deserving of our praise and reverence, this subject alone could easily fill our whole time of prayer!

We should long for his kingdom to expand among us: "Your kingdom come, your will be done, on earth as it is in heaven" (Matt 6:10). How earnestly concerned are we about seeing the kingdom of God expand? In light of our current study, doesn't this petition encourage us to ask others to love him as we do?

We should also in our prayer raise our petitions to him: "Give us each day our daily bread." Note that this prayer points to grace sufficient for today — not grace sufficient for the week or month ahead! This is evocative of the manna that fell from heaven and fed God's people day by day in the wilderness (cf. Exod 16).

We should confess our sins: "Forgive us our sins, for we also forgive everyone who sins against us." Thomas Pollock aptly wrote:

> We have not loved Thee as we ought,
> Nor cared that we are loved by Thee;
> Thy presence we have coldly sought,
> And feebly longed Thy face to see.
> Lord, give a pure and loving heart
> To feel and know the love Thou art."[1]

Finally, we should seek to *overcome* sin: "Lead us not into temptation."

All of this may seem familiar to you. But given the pace of life and the manifold competing demands we all face, we must ask: Am I taking time to pray in this kind of well-rounded way? Are my prayers rushed or half-hearted? Is my prayer focused primarily on intimacy with my God, or is it focused instead on my needs and interests? Is my prayer an act of humility, love, and submission or an expression of desires?

Also, while it is a wonderful thing to pray on one's own, should we not seek to be in prayer with others as well? Jesus said, "Again, truly I tell you that if two of you on earth agree about anything you ask for, it will be done for them by my Father in heaven. For where two or three gather in my name, there am I with them" (Matt 18:19–20). While this counsel is not clearly restricted to prayer, it is certainly applicable.

As such, we see glorious examples of individual prayer recorded in Scripture (such as Daniel 9), but also incredible testimonies of congregational prayer (e.g., 1 Kings 8; Ezra 9; Nehemiah 9). The frequency of our corporate prayer may be a sign of the relative health of our congregations. Revival in the churches in Korea, for example, has often been connected to the prayer meetings that precipitated the revival.

chapter 6

GIVING

THERE IS NO ACT OF CHRISTIAN WORSHIP that can be so easily faked as giving. One might give vast sums of money to "the church" but have no genuine love for God. By contrast, perhaps the most important illustration in giving that we find in all Scripture relates to one of the smallest contributions ever recorded:

> Jesus sat down opposite the place where the offerings were put and watched the crowd putting their money into the temple treasury. Many rich people threw in large amounts. But a poor widow came and put in two very small copper coins, worth only a few cents.
>
> Calling his disciples to him, Jesus said, "Truly I tell you, this poor widow has put more into the treasury than all the others. They all gave out of their wealth; but she, out of her poverty, put in everything — all she had to live on." (Mark 12:41 – 44)

In this light, we should understand that the Word of God penetrates even the "thoughts and attitudes of the heart" (Heb 4:12b). While mechanically it may be easy to give, it can be no small challenge to give in a way that pleases God.

That said, in most congregations, the bigger problem seems to be that too few people give at all. We sing the old hymn "Take My Life and Let It Be" and declare, "Take my silver and my gold, not a mite would I withhold." But all the while, a substantial proportion of our congregation has in fact done this very thing, withholding their "silver and gold."

Now, it is easy for us to make excuses for ourselves:

- The economy is bad.
- I'm between jobs.
- I don't earn much.
- I earn too much to tithe.
- I can't afford it.
- I don't think there are any commands in the Bible that are clear on this.

Every year, when we do our taxes, we see a scorecard with respect to our giving; that is, we consider our so-called "charitable giving." Have we obeyed the apostle Paul? "Therefore, I urge you, brothers and sisters, in view of God's mercy, to offer your bodies as living sacrifices, holy and pleasing to God — this is your true and proper worship" (Rom 12:1). We talk about laying our all on the altar for God, but when Paul talks here about offering our bodies as "living sacrifices," surely he's not talking about any kind of *monetary* sacrifice, is he?

More specifically, Paul wrote to the Corinthians, "Each of you should give what you have decided in your heart to give, not reluctantly or under compulsion, for God loves a cheerful giver" (2 Cor 9:7). People who love God give to the causes that stir the heart of God. The Bible talks often about gifts, tithes, and offerings. We enjoy spending money freely on the things we love. What does our giving — the giving we did in the last week, month, or year — tell us about our love for God in comparison to our love for other things? In the gospel of Luke, we read about a woman who had "lived a sinful life" (Luke 7:37). She has come to love Jesus, recognizing that she had been forgiven of much, and the Scripture says, she has "great love" (Luke 7:47). By our giving, we can ask ourselves: Do we love little, or much?

chapter 7

LOVE *for* OTHERS

BECAUSE JESUS TAUGHT that the second great commandment — "Love your neighbor as yourself" — was "like" the first great commandment, we might assume that, over the course of church history, there would have been nearly as equal an emphasis on this commandment as there was on the first, where we are called to love the Lord our God with all our heart, soul, and mind.

In the first section of this book, we considered the first great commandment and some of the ways in which we can live it out. As we consider our own lives, we need to reflect on this issue and determine firmly to honor the reality of the second great commandment as an extension of the first. The apostle John sets the challenge before us starkly: "Dear friends, let us love one another, for love comes from God. Everyone who loves has been born of God and knows God. Whoever does not love does not know God, because God is love" (1 John 4:7-8).

In a familiar story in our Gospels, we find a man who was an expert in the law of God puzzled at one crucial point. He wondered who his "neighbor" was (Luke 10:29-37). The very question reveals the man's heart. He thought that by narrowing the field of humanity down to a manageable subset (i.e., one's family, the people in one's church, the people in one's religious circles, etc.), the idea of loving one's neighbor might be more palatable.

Let's face it: there are some human beings who are unpleasant to be around. There are people in our world with poor hygiene. There are people in our world who look scary. There are people in our lives against whom we might hold prejudices (even subconsciously). There are people in our world who have hurt us or those we love. It's true, isn't it? We *want* to narrow the meaning of this phrase down. In the Sermon on the Mount, Jesus addressed this directly:

> You have heard that it was said, "Love your neighbor and hate your enemy." But I tell you, love your enemies and pray for those who persecute you, that you may be children of your Father in heaven. He causes his sun to rise on the evil and the good, and sends rain on the righteous and the unrighteous. If you love those who love you, what reward will you get? Are not even the tax collectors doing that? And if you greet only your own people, what are you doing more than others? Do not even pagans do that? Be perfect, therefore, as your heavenly Father is perfect. (Matt 5:43 – 48)

On that day when the man asked Jesus who his neighbor was, he was voicing aloud the question that we ourselves may have furtively hidden in our own hearts. If we're being honest with ourselves, at times it's hard to love even the most lovable people in our lives. Our cranky son. Our whining daughter. The husband or wife who wakes up with morning breath. Our mom or dad who simply will not see the wisdom of our choices.

Our all-knowing brother. Our sister who needs just one more favor. Our pushy boyfriend. Our too-often late girlfriend.

Often, on our desks or in a thousand electronic forms, we keep pictures of our closest loved ones nearby. The danger with these images is simple: they are quiet, peaceful, and perfect. The reality of life is that, because of all the sinful people, even those we love the most are hard to love at times.

Jesus calls us to a self-sacrificing love that pushes us past our comfort zone into a world of risk and danger. His answer to the question, "Who is my neighbor?" was this well-known but too rarely internalized parable:

> "A man was going down from Jerusalem to Jericho, when he was attacked by robbers. They stripped him of his clothes, beat him and went away, leaving him half dead. A priest happened to be going down the same road, and when he saw the man, he passed by on the other side. So too, a Levite, when he came to the place and saw him, passed by on the other side. But a Samaritan, as he traveled, came where the man was; and when he saw him, he took pity on him. He went to him and bandaged his wounds, pouring on oil and wine. Then he put the man on his own donkey, brought him to an inn and took care of him. The next day he took out two denarii and gave them to the innkeeper. 'Look after him,' he said, 'and when I return, I will reimburse you for any extra expense you may have.'
>
> Which of these three do you think was a neighbor to the man who fell into the hands of robbers?"
>
> The expert in the law replied, "The one who had mercy on him."
>
> Jesus told him, "Go and do likewise." (Luke 10:30–37)

It is a well-documented fact of history that Jews in the first-century did not get along with Samaritans. As such, when Jesus identified the hero in this story as a Samaritan (as opposed to the seemingly righteous priest or Levite), he was crafting a lesson that would cross all social boundaries.

We are told in countless ways — by our families, by society, by the media, by our friends, and even by our churches — to remember to be *safe*. Safety has, for many, become a god. We have insurance policies for every imaginable malady that can befall a human being. We have the option to purchase contracts that protect the most trivial gadgets we can buy. We organize our lives to minimize pain and risk. But Jesus is here thundering against all claims to safety and comfort and is calling us to "go and do likewise." Go to that man, to that woman, whom no one else will care for. Pour out even your own wealth and substance for the Samaritan in your life, the one you would least naturally reach out to, and sacrifice your time, money, and even your own well-being.

In the same way that in the first section of this book I encouraged you to pause and reflect, I will ask you to do so now: pause for a moment and pray about this. I confess that when I read books and authors that ask us to do such things, I am rarely willing to do what they suggest. Despite this, I urge you to take a moment now, get out a piece of paper, and reflect on the call to love our neighbor as ourselves. Ponder these questions: What does this commandment mean to you now? What should it mean? What will you do differently? To whom do you need to reach out? What have you been afraid to attempt? Pray. Write down your responses. Determine to make changes.

One of my favorite characters in Scripture is a man

named Caleb. He went into enemy territory along with Joshua and ten other spies. While these ten other spies saw only how large the enemies were, Joshua and Caleb held a different view. And Caleb said, "We should go up and take possession of the land, for we can certainly do it" (Num 13:30b). What will love for our neighbor look like in our lives if we share this same perspective?

chapter 8

THE LIFE OF SERVICE LEADS *to* OPPORTUNITIES *for* EVANGELISM AND MISSIONS

EVANGELISM IS OFTEN DISCUSSED in our Christian circles — as it should be. The two passages we turn to most commonly in discussions about evangelism come readily to mind. First, in a passage that is so famous that we have a name for it — the Great Commission — we read this command from Jesus: "Therefore go and make disciples of all nations, baptizing them in the name of the Father and of the Son and of the Holy Spirit, and teaching them to obey everything I have commanded you. And surely I am with you always, to the very end of the age" (Matt 28:19 – 20). Second, just before his ascension into heaven, Jesus commanded the disciples (and, we assume, us as well): "But you will receive power when the Holy Spirit comes on you; and you will be my witnesses in Jerusalem, and

in all Judea and Samaria, and to the ends of the earth"
(Acts 1:8).

Sharing our faith with others is something that our
God has emphatically commanded. Even more, the reality of heaven and hell presses us to love our neighbors
by warning them about the consequences of the decisions they make in this life. But for our own part, we
hear dire warnings in Scripture: if we fail to share the
truth with those in our lives who are apart from Christ,
as the prophet Ezekiel put it, their blood is on our hands
(cf. Ezek 3:16–21). Rather than viewing this as a burden-
some responsibility, we should receive with great joy the
idea that we have the privilege to share with others the
glories of our God in Christ. Jesus is that "rose of Sha-
ron" (Song 2:1), whose sweet savor fills the world with
goodness and gladness. Surely, evangelism should be an
effortless, natural aspect of the Christian life.

Surely, we should all have in mind an approach to
sharing our faith that comes readily to mind, so that
as the opportunity presents itself, we are able to easily share the gospel of life. As Peter suggests, "In your
hearts revere Christ as Lord. Always be prepared to give
an answer to everyone who asks you to give the reason
for the hope that you have. But do this with gentleness
and respect" (1 Pet 3:15). I have always favored the simple rubric ABC in this capacity as I have shared what the
gospel means with others:

A (Admit) — Admit that you are a sinner. Romans
3:23 is often pointed to as a great text that
illustrates our need to understand that we are
all indeed sinners. Paul writes, "All have sinned
and fall short of the glory of God." He adds in
Romans 6:23, "The wages of sin is death, but
the gift of God is eternal life in Christ Jesus our

Lord." We have all earned judgment for our sins, but there is hope in Jesus Christ.

B (Believe) — We are called to believe in Jesus — in his deity, his coming to earth, his sinless life, his suffering and crucifixion, his death, and his resurrection. This is the heart of the gospel. We read "that Christ died for our sins according to the Scriptures, that he was buried, that he was raised on the third day according to the Scriptures" (1 Cor 15:3b – 4).

C (Commit) — If we have genuinely admitted that we are imperfect, sinful creatures and if we have believed in all that is said in Scripture about Jesus, our faith must not end there. Such mere faith, James asserts, is dead and useless (cf. Jas 2:14 – 24). By contrast, if we have trusted in Jesus for eternal life, we should commit our lives completely to him. Jesus said, "If anyone comes to me and does not hate father and mother, wife and children, brothers and sisters — yes, even their own life — such a person cannot be my disciple. And anyone who does not carry their cross and follow me cannot be my disciple" (Luke 14:26 – 27).

As an aside, it is urgently important to emphasize this one plain fact: if you yourself have never admitted your sin, believed in Jesus, or committed your life wholly to him, you must do so! Your first act of evangelism must be spoken to your own soul in order to be an effective evangelist!

In practice, evangelism has proven to be challenging, even though the facts of the gospel are as simple as ABC. If we desire to be *effective* evangelists rather than mere evangelists, we may need to reflect soberly on what might be wrong with our approach. Consider a few of the common ways evangelism has been taught in recent years, held before the church as examples of how we should share our faith.

The Master Plan of Evangelism.[1] This approach considers the life of Jesus and how it was that Jesus poured his life into the disciples closest to him. Similarly, we are called to model the life of Christianity for others and in this way multiply genuine disciples. In this approach, it is seen as better to give one's life to key individuals who can, in turn, give their lives away calling others to Christ.

Out of the Salt Shaker and into the World.[2] In Matthew 5:13, Jesus refers to believers as the "salt of the earth." Becky Pippert uses this image to suggest that Christians need to get out of their churches and into the world. Evangelism is too often feared by the church and, at times, by the targets of our evangelism, and our approach should instead be natural and winsome. Evangelism should indeed be a lifestyle.

The Four Spiritual Laws.[3] This widely influential tract has been produced in many different languages and has been used by many as a tool that can be passed along to others as they seek to consider the claims of Christ. This tract asserts that "God has a wonderful plan for your life," and we must ultimately remove ourselves from the "throne" of our self-directed lives, receive Christ as Savior, and give him the throne.

Evangelism Explosion.[4] This method of sharing the faith encourages believers to begin conversations with prospective converts with probing questions: "Have you come to a place in your spiritual journey where you know that if you were to die tonight, you would go to heaven?" Second, one might ask, "If God were to ask you, 'Why should I let you into my heaven?' what would you say?"

Hear me well: all of these approaches have potential merit. Whether you appreciate the simplicity of the ABC approach to sharing the Christian faith that I have outlined, or one of these other methods, or any of the many others that exist, we must carefully consider an aspect of sharing our faith that is too rarely considered when we discuss evangelism: *combining our efforts to share the gospel with Christian service will improve our effectiveness.* Remember Jesus' parable of the good Samaritan. Surely, the man on the road to Jericho would have been open to listening to anything the Samaritan had to say, since he alone had cared for him (even at great personal cost) when others had been unwilling to do so.

By contrast, where evangelism is taking place in our churches, we might go to the homes of those who have visited our church or go door to door in the neighborhoods around our churches. It almost seems as if our evangelistic approaches are designed for traditional, suburban communities: we go and visit people like us and try to make the experience nonthreatening, while still coming to the point. We bring cookies, perhaps.

On the surface, does this mirror well the approach to outreach that Jesus lived out? We see him out in the world seeking out hurting people. Touching the leper. Caring for the sick. Spending time with tax collectors and sinners. And talking to the Samaritan woman at the well who had a checkered past. Why are we surprised that people who live in expensive homes are resistant to the gospel? They believe they have everything they need! If, however, we were to couple our efforts to evangelize with acts of Christian mercy, how much more genuine might our testimony be?

Of course, this is not to say that we should not also be reaching out to the homes around our churches, or to witness to those who visit our congregations, or to testify to those who may be rich in the things of this world, but are poor spiritually. But we must do more. By virtue of the examples we find in Scripture, we might be surprised at how much more effective our outreach might be if we intentionally seek to show love to those our society thinks of as unlovable. But how would we get started?

chapter 9

LOVING *the* NEIGHBORS NEAR OUR HOMES

THERE ARE TWO KEY IDEAS for us to begin with as we consider working with those who are in need near where we live: *opportunity* and *attitude*. First, let's consider *opportunity*. Wherever we are, as Christians we are either a part of churches seeking to make a difference, or we are individuals trying to do our part in serving the Lord. But the opportunities that we all have are radically different. Paul wrote to the churches in Galatia, "Therefore, as we have opportunity, let us do good to all people, especially to those who belong to the family of believers" (Gal 6:10). We should be actively seeking out opportunities to serve. But consider three different settings where your ministry might take place.

You live in a busy American city. In most cities, even a small apartment can be expensive. Churches often struggle to make the budget, often eking out an existence. Attracting church staff can be a challenge. There are rough parts of town where there are few churches. If you travel a few blocks in one direction or another, the landscape can go from upscale urban professional to grimy and impoverished. You might see homeless folks holding a coffee cup from an expensive designer coffee boutique. Traffic, noise, and distractions are a constant. That said, there is often a seeming electricity to life in the city; there's always something to do or see, and it's often exciting to explore other parts of the city even when you've been living there for a long time.

You live in a middle-class, suburban neighborhood. Churches often thrive in suburban settings; whether small or large, our churches are used as voting stations, are borrowed by homeowner associations, and serve as home to weddings and funerals. While there is a wide variation depending on whether your church is in the northern, southern, eastern, or western part of the country, suburban churches are used to having people come and go as they move in or out. In most suburban churches, everyone looks and sounds basically the same; there is less ethnic and social diversity than one might find in some urban churches. Suburban churches generally have their pick of which ministers might be willing to come and serve.

You live in a rural community. Many churches that are a part of rural settings have been in place for a long time. If you go to many rural churches, you will find that there are two or three family names that often appear routinely within the congregation. A church social almost always involves food and customarily is a potluck supper. When a visitor comes into the church, usually all of the regulars know it. It can be as hard to find a pastor who is willing to come and serve in a rural setting as it is for many urban churches to find qualified staff. Often, someone who is just getting started in ministry might be willing to come or, perhaps, a minister who is getting somewhat old for the profession.

While each of these three settings is a stereotypical caricature of what you might find in a church located in a city, a suburb, or a rural community, this does illustrate an important point: each of us is a part of very different communities, and the opportunities that we have for service will be radically different depending on the community we serve. Before considering the implications of this further, let's consider the second key idea associated with this topic: *attitude*.

Many have taken the statement Jesus made in Matthew 26:11 — "The poor you will always have with you" — and used it as an excuse to do little or nothing for others. But this statement follows closely after Jesus' parable of the sheep and the goats. The sheep (those who would inherit eternal life) and the goats (those who would not inherit eternal life) are divided based on the character of their lives lived out in service to others. When Jesus taught that the poor would always be with us, he was emphasizing that he himself would soon be crucified. His time on earth was brief. By contrast, there will always be people who are poor in our world. Can we really use such a statement to justify our sloth?

Our attitude about caring for the needs of other human beings ultimately determines how effective we will be as evangelists. We must have an attitude whereby we are constantly looking for needs wherever they may be. Within our homes, outside our front door, in our neighborhood, or in our travels, we must not simply be looking for "divine appointments" to share the gospel; we must be looking for divine appointments to serve. Whenever and wherever we are able to care for another human being and show genuine love, we have a glorious occasion to express why we are showing love: "We love because he first loved us" (1 John 4:19). L. Shannon

Jung shares an account that we can perhaps all relate to, which illustrates well how challenging it is to show such love, but also how such challenges can be overcome:

> My morning route to Saint Paul School of Theology takes me past a QT gas station. The gas is a bit cheaper there and so I often stop. Early in the morning you can find quite a collection of people at the station.... [One] is an old woman whose shoes have seen much better days. This woman is gray-haired and wrinkled, and she often wears a worn gray sweatshirt and a nondescript skirt. She usually stands about five feet inside the door, looking as if she does not know where she is and certainly not where she is going.
>
> I'll admit that I don't like seeing this woman, and I try to distance myself from her.... I do not know her history. What sort of housing can she afford? What does she eat? Does she have a job? Does it have benefits? And how does her experience benefit me? She threatens my sense of well-being. But she is also the possibility of relationship and renewed well-being.[1]

I appreciate this author's honesty and openness. We as Christians talk often about men and women like Lottie Moon or Hudson Taylor going to China, or George Müller's prayer life and his work among the orphans, and we make much about the evangelistic success of men like D. L. Moody or Billy Graham. But genuine Christian faith can be a far messier thing. It requires us to look at the routine, unspectacular, and at times uncomfortable aspects of our lives and cross the great gulf between ourselves and another human being: the one right in front of us.

The problem is not *finding* the needs of people in our

lives; the problem is *caring* enough to act in a manner that is far different than perhaps we have acted previously. We must show love to the loveless. We must be Christ to the one without Christ. When Jesus encountered such people in the Gospels, he did not merely talk to them from a distance; rather, he touched them. By contrast, we too often count it a great victory if we throw a quarter from our barely open window in the direction of the homeless man. We have opportunities. Will we have a renewed attitude? Paul wrote:

> In your relationships with one another, have the same mindset as Christ Jesus:
>
>> Who, being in very nature God,
>>> did not consider equality with God something to be used to his own advantage;
>> rather, he made himself nothing
>>> by taking the very nature of a servant,
>>> being made in human likeness.
>> And being found in appearance as a man,
>>> he humbled himself
>>> by becoming obedient to death —
>>>> even death on a cross! (Phil 2:5 – 11)

chapter 10

LOVING OUR NEIGHBOR ELSEWHERE

IN THE LAST SECTION, we considered the importance of serving others near our homes. Now, we need to look not only beyond our own doorstep but also well beyond our comfort zones. You'll recall that Acts 1:8, one of the two most frequently cited verses on evangelism, teaches, "But you will receive power when the Holy Spirit comes on you; and you will be my witnesses in Jerusalem, and in all Judea and Samaria, and to the ends of the earth." In this statement Jesus, just prior to his ascension into heaven, reinforces the work that his disciples are to be engaged in. As we receive this commandment where we live, we've already considered in the previous chapter the importance of the "Jerusalem" and "Judea" in this statement as to how we might help our neighbors. Now we need to consider "Samaria" and "the ends of the earth."

One of the reasons this passage pushes us out of our comfort zone can be seen in this word "Samaria." We have already observed that the Samaritans and Jews were natural enemies. For Jesus to urge his disciples specifically to consider the Samaritans required the desciples to undertake not only a physical journey, but also a cultural one. Perhaps a useful starting point for us would be to consider how we might paraphrase such a command as Americans. Perhaps we might hear something like this: "But you will receive power when the Holy Spirit comes on you; and you will be my witnesses where you live, and throughout the state and nation, and in Iraq or Afghanistan, and to the ends of the earth." Samaria would have been a place where the message of someone from the Jewish people might likely have met with opposition. Shouldn't we acknowledge that this is an element of the commandment that God has for us here?

By contrast, the missionary impulse seems at low ebb in our age. We Christians seem afraid of our own shadows. Let's be specific: consider going to a place where proclaiming Jesus Christ might be most challenging, as, for example, in a country such as Yemen. There are travel challenges to contend with. There are likely political realities to consider, even in obtaining legal access to the country; depending on where we were born, our passport may not be viewed as a positive. Assuming we make it into the country, we have language barriers. Do we even know what language or languages are spoken there? Could we read a street sign? One thing we do know is that the people of Yemen have not shown great openness to anyone sharing the gospel of Jesus Christ among them. There would be far more than casual social opposition to deal with; the risks could be physical and the consequences permanent. But millions of people live in Yemen. Who will share the truths of our Savior with the people of Yemen?

But Yemen is by no means the only country to which a Christian might travel that is hostile to the gospel. Hundreds of millions of people live in countries where their government considers the preaching of the Word a hostile act for which one should be imprisoned. John Piper once put it this way:

> The price is suffering, and the volatility in the world today against the church is not decreasing. It is increasing, especially among the groups that need the gospel. There is no such thing as a closed country. It's a foreign notion. It has no root or warrant in the Bible, and it would have been unintelligible to the apostle Paul who laid down his life in every city he went to. Therefore, there are martyrs in this room.
>
> Statistically it's easy to predict. One Sunday recently there was a focus on the suffering church, and many of you were involved in it. This World Missions Fellowship was involved in it, and you all saw videos or heard stories about places like Sudan where the Muslim regime is systematically ostracizing, positioning, and starving Christians so that there are about 500 martyrs a day there....
>
> Now this is exactly the opposite of what I hear mainly in America as people decide where to live, for example. I don't hear people saying, "I don't want to leave, because this is where I'm called to and this is where there's need." Would you please join me in reversing American evangelical priorities? It seems to be woven into the very fabric of our consumer culture that we move toward comfort, toward security, toward ease, toward safety, away from stress, away from trouble, and away from danger. It ought to be exactly the opposite! "He who would come after me let him take up his cross and die!"[1]

Thus, we must each consider how to reach "Samaria" in our own age. It will likely hurt. If you've ever succeeded on a diet, you know that the restraint required hurts. In a spiritual sense, we need to go on a diet as well, combating our flesh and embracing even suffering and sacrifice. But in addition, the commandment Jesus gave the disciples looked beyond Samaria "to the ends of the earth."

In the history of humankind, the church has never had better opportunities to obey this commandment than it does now. Even up until the beginning of the nineteenth century, most people never traveled more than a few miles from their homes. While it's true that many people even in our age are homebodies, in many countries, getting on a plane or in a car and traveling to various places is routine. Many people vacation in countries other than the one they live in at least once or even many times in their lives. Business travel sends men and women around the world. Student exchange programs are increasingly commonplace.

As a result, most Christian churches have a clear awareness of short-term missions opportunities domestically and abroad. We have no excuse: going to "the ends of the earth" seems to be a commandment particularly tailored to our age.

But what might we do while there? We know that, regardless of how we serve, sharing the gospel in every setting is an essential dimension to true missions. In addition, though, what kinds of activities that we might support will help grow the spiritual fruit we hope to harvest? This is the topic of the last chapter.

chapter 11

AREAS *of* POSSIBLE CHRISTIAN SERVICE

AS WE CONSIDER WAYS in which we can be "loving our neighbor as ourselves" in local and global settings, it's urgently important to discuss and participate in specific paths of service. Talk is cheap. While serving others has often been an area of strength for the Christian church, in recent days such service often seems to have fallen out of vogue. Cathy Butler writes.

> Throughout church history, Christians have been on the forefront of changing society with hospitals, schools, orphanages, and other institutions to minister to the poor and those in need. Now, for a variety of reasons, the church is sometimes running behind society; observe the church's slow response to the AIDS epidemic. Now we run the risk of needing the world to lead us to the areas of great human need, rather than taking the lead in transforming our culture by ministering to the poor in the name of Christ. When those who do not know Christ do a better job of championing justice and bestowing mercy than do Christ's followers,

the church's witness to the gospel is damaged and
weakened.[1]

It is biblical to reach out and serve others, as this
section will demonstrate. Put another way, God has
emphatically urged all of his people to minister his
love to a hurting world. We often hear Christians pray
for revival and talk passionately about how they long to
see many souls converted, but the connection between
Christian service and the salvation of the lost is intimately related. Even more, our Christian service is genuine evidence, perhaps above all things, of our love for
God. We are urged to "find out what pleases the Lord"
(Eph 5:10). The suggestions that follow are intended to
provide a few paths to discovering the kinds of things
that are pleasing to God, both for ourselves and for the
churches we are a part of.

One word of warning. The information that follows
should be considered a distillation of a wide range of
teachings we find in Scripture about service, something
I like to refer to as evangelical mercy ministry. Some of
the topics listed are not traditionally mentioned in such
discussions. It would be wrong to simply read quickly
through this list of possible activities for service and
never to pause for prayer or reflection, asking, "In what
ways might I serve the Lord by serving others?"

In addition, you should also be praying that the Lord
might reveal *other* ways whereby you might serve that
are not mentioned in this review. Remember: it was
the Holy Spirit that God's people were to rely on when
they proceeded from "Jerusalem, and in all Judea and
Samaria, and to the ends of the earth" (Acts 1:8b). Many
of the passages that follow are encouraging, but others
are rebukes. May the Lord use his Word to convict and
challenge us.

Please note: for a couple of the issues in this list, I fully expect that the connection between the topic and the supporting Scripture may not be obvious. Look at the verse cited in context. Prayerfully reflect on the topic and the biblical text. Ask yourself, "Are there other passages that teach us something about this topic?" This is the portion of the book I am hoping you will read most carefully, featuring as it does the Word of God.

Feed the Hungry

"Whoever shuts their ears to the cry of the poor will also cry out and not be answered" (Prov 21:13).

"The generous will themselves be blessed, for they share their food with the poor" (Prov 22:9).

"Whoever increases wealth by taking interest or profit from the poor amasses it for another, who will be kind to the poor" (Prov 28:8).

"Those who give to the poor will lack nothing, but those who close their eyes to them receive many curses" (Prov 28:27).

Fight Famine

"Have I not wept for those in trouble? Has not my soul grieved for the poor?" (Job 30:25).

"The poor will eat and be satisfied; those who seek the LORD will praise him — may your hearts live forever!" (Ps 22:26).

"Her poor I will satisfy with food" (Ps 132:15b).

"An unplowed field produces food for the poor, but injustice sweeps it away" (Prov 13:23).

Give Drink to the Thirsty

"I was thirsty and you gave me something to drink" (Matt 25:35b).

"If your enemy is hungry, give him food to eat; if he is thirsty, give him water to drink" (Prov 25:21).

"The poor and needy search for water, but there is none; their tongues are parched with thirst. But I the LORD will answer them; I, the God of Israel, will not forsake them. I will make rivers flow on barren heights, and springs within the valleys. I will turn the desert into pools of water, and the parched ground into springs" (Isa 41:17 – 18).

Care for the Stranger

"Do not mistreat or oppress him a foreigner, for you were foreigners in Egypt" (Exod 22:21; this exact thought is expressed in numerous other passages).

"I took up the case of the stranger" (Job 29:16b).

"The people of the land practice extortion and commit robbery; they oppress the poor and needy and mistreat the foreigner, denying them justice" (Ezek 22:29).

Help the Homeless

"He raises the poor from the dust and lifts the needy from the ash heap; he seats them with princes, with the princes of his people" (Ps 113:7 – 8).

"Whoever oppresses the poor shows contempt for their Maker, but whoever is kind to the needy honors God" (Prov 14:31).

"Whoever is kind to the poor lends to the LORD, and he will reward them for what they have done" (Prov 19:17).

"Rich and poor have this in common: The LORD is the Maker of them all" (Prov 22:2).

Supply Clothes to the Needy

"I needed clothes and you clothed me" (Matt 25:36a).

Care for the Sick

"I was sick and you looked after me" (Matt 25:36b).

"Wealth attracts many friends, but even the closest friend of the poor person deserts them" (Prov 19:4).

"The poor are shunned by all their relatives — how much more do their friends avoid them! Though the poor pursue them with pleading, they are nowhere to be found" (Prov 19:7).

"If someone curses their father or mother, their lamp will be snuffed out in pitch darkness" (Prov 20:20).

"Listen to your father, who gave you life, and do not despise your mother when she is old" (Prov 23:22).

"Like a broken tooth or a lame foot is reliance on the unfaithful in a time of trouble" (Prov 25:19).

Provide Disaster Relief

"You have been a refuge for the poor, a refuge for the needy in their distress, a shelter from the storm and a shade from the heat" (Isa 25:4a).

Minister to the Imprisoned

"I was in prison and you came to visit me" (Matt 25:36c).

"The LORD hears the needy and does not despise his captive people" (Ps 69:33).

"Whoever mocks the poor shows contempt for their Maker" (Prov 17:5a).

Balancing notions: "Do not show favoritism to a poor person in his lawsuit" (Exod 23:3) and "It is not good to be partial to the wicked and so deprive the innocent of justice" (Prov 18:5).

"Do not gloat when your enemy falls; when they stumble, do not let your heart rejoice, or the LORD will see and disapprove and turn his wrath away from them" (Prov 24:17 – 18).

"The righteous care about justice for the poor, but the wicked have no such concern" (Prov 29:7).

"If a king judges the poor with fairness, his throne will be established forever" (Prov 29:14).

Effectively Oppose Abortion

"'Because the poor are plundered and the needy groan, I will now arise,' says the LORD. 'I will protect them from those who malign them'" (Ps 12:5).

"If you say, 'But we knew nothing about this,' does not he who weighs the heart perceive it? Does not he who guards your life know it? Will he not repay everyone according to what they have done?" (Prov 24:12).

"Speak up for those who cannot speak for themselves, for the rights of all who are destitute. Speak up and judge fairly; defend the rights of the poor and needy" (Prov 31:8 – 9).

Offer Crisis Pregnancy Support

"Do not withhold good from those to whom it is due, when it is in your power to act. Do not say to your neighbor, 'Come back tomorrow and I'll give it to you — when you already have it with you" (Prov 3:27 – 28).

Adopt

"Whoever heard me spoke well of me, and those who saw me commended me, because I rescued the poor who cried for help, and the fatherless who had none to assist him" (Job 29:11 – 12).

"May he defend the afflicted among the people and save the children of the needy; may he crush the oppressor" (Ps 72:4).

"Defend the weak and the fatherless; uphold the cause of the poor and the oppressed" (Ps 82:3).

"Religion that God our Father accepts as pure and faultless is this: to look after orphans and widows in their distress and to keep oneself from being polluted by the world" (Jas 1:27).

Be a Foster Parent

"She opens her arms to the poor and extends her hands to the needy" (Prov 31:20).

"I was a father to the needy" (Job 29:16a).

Fight Child Abuse

"Do not let the oppressed retreat in disgrace; may the poor and needy praise your name" (Ps 74:21).

"It is God's will that you should be sanctified: that you should avoid sexual immorality; that each of you should learn to control your own body in a way that is holy and honorable, not in passionate lust like the pagans, who do not know God; and that in this matter no one should wrong or take advantage of a brother or sister. The Lord will punish all those who commit such sins, as we told you and warned you before. For God did not call us to be impure, but to live a holy life. Therefore, anyone who rejects this instruction does not reject a human being but God, the very God who gives you his Holy Spirit" (1 Thess 4:3–8).

Fight Pornography

"Treat younger men as brothers, older women as mothers, and younger women as sisters, with absolute purity" (1 Tim 5:1b–2).

Support Women's Shelters

"But let all who take refuge in you be glad; let them ever sing for joy. Spread your protection over them, that those who love your name may rejoice in you" (Ps 5:11).

"Whoever dwells in the shelter of the Most High will rest in the shadow of the Almighty. I will say of the LORD, 'He is my refuge and my fortress, my God, in whom I trust.' Surely he will save you from the fowler's snare and from the deadly pestilence. He will cover you with his feathers, and under his wings you will find refuge; his faithfulness will be your shield and rampart" (Ps 91:1 – 4).

Care for Widows

"I made the widow's heart sing" (Job 29:13b).

"Woe to those who make unjust laws, to those who issue oppressive decrees, to deprive the poor of their rights and withhold justice from the oppressed of my people, making widows their prey and robbing the fatherless. What will you do on the day of reckoning, when disaster comes from afar? To whom will you run for help? Where will you leave your riches?" (Isa 10:1 – 3).

"In Joppa there was a disciple named Tabitha (in Greek her name is Dorcas); she was always doing good and helping the poor. About that time she became sick and died, and her body was washed and placed in an upstairs room. Lydda was near Joppa; so when the disciples heard that Peter was in Lydda, they sent two men to him and urged him, "Please come at once!"

Peter went with them, and when he arrived he was taken upstairs to the room. All the widows stood around him, crying and showing him the robes and other clothing that Dorcas had made while she was still with them" (Acts 9:36 – 40).

Care for the Disabled

"The poor are shunned even by their neighbors, but the rich have many friends. It is a sin to despise one's neighbor, but blessed is the one who is kind to the needy" (Prov 14:20–21).

"In a very short time, will not Lebanon be turned into a fertile field and the fertile field seem like a forest? In that day the deaf will hear the words of the scroll, and out of gloom and darkness the eyes of the blind will see. Once more the humble will rejoice in the LORD; the needy will rejoice in the Holy One of Israel" (Isa 29:17–19).

"Then Jesus said to his host, 'When you give a luncheon or dinner, do not invite your friends, your brothers or sisters, your relatives, or your rich neighbors; if you do, they may invite you back and so you will be repaid. But when you give a banquet, invite the poor, the crippled, the lame, the blind, and you will be blessed. Although they cannot repay you, you will be repaid at the resurrection of the righteous'" (Luke 14:12–14).

"In everything I did, I showed you that by this kind of hard work we must help the weak, remembering the words the Lord Jesus himself said: 'It is more blessed to give than to receive'" (Acts 20:35).

"And we urge you, brothers and sisters, warn those who are idle and disruptive, encourage the disheartened, help the weak, be patient with everyone" (1 Thess 5:14).

Give Hospice Care

"The one who was dying blessed me" (Job 29:13a).

Fight for Human Rights

"You rescue the poor from those too strong for them, the poor and needy from those who rob them" (Ps 35:10b).

"Sing to the LORD! Give praise to the LORD! He rescues the life of the needy from the hands of the wicked" (Jer 20:13).

Fight Racism

"But let justice roll on like a river, righteousness like a never-failing stream!" (Amos 5:24).

Fight Drug and Alcohol Abuse

"Israel, put your hope in the LORD, for with the LORD is unfailing love and with him is full redemption" (Ps 130:7).

"Wine is a mocker and beer a brawler; whoever is led astray by them is not wise" (Prov 20:1).

"There is surely a future hope for you, and your hope will not be cut off" (Prov 23:18).

Fight for Fair Wages

"Do not take advantage of a hired worker who is poor and needy, whether that worker is a fellow Israelite or a foreigner residing in one of your towns. Pay them their wages each day before sunset, because they are poor and are counting on it. Otherwise they may cry to the LORD against you, and you will be guilty of sin" (Deut 24:14-15).

Fight for Health Care Reform

"Whoever pursues righteousness and love finds life, prosperity and honor" (Prov 21:21).

Teach Financial Responsibility

"If you lend money to one of my people among you who is needy, do not treat it like a business deal; charge no interest" (Exod 22:25).

"If anyone is poor among your fellow Israelites in any of the towns of the land the LORD your God is giving you, do not be hardhearted or tightfisted toward them. Rather, be openhanded and freely lend them whatever they need" (Deut 15:7–8).

"For even when we were with you, we gave you this rule: 'The one who is unwilling to work shall not eat'" (2 Thess 3:10).

Enter the Political Arena

"At this, the administrators and the satraps tried to find grounds for charges against Daniel in his conduct of government affairs, but they were unable to do so. They could find no corruption in him, because he was trustworthy and neither corrupt nor negligent" (Dan 6:4).

Be Outspoken

"He will take pity on the weak and the needy and save the needy from death. He will rescue them from oppression and violence, for precious is their blood in his sight" (Ps 72:13–14).

Go Somewhere No One Else Is Willing to Go

"But God will never forget the needy; the hope of the afflicted will never perish" (Ps 9:18).

Live Unselfishly

"One person gives freely, yet gains even more; another withholds unduly, but comes to poverty. A generous person will prosper; whoever refreshes others will be refreshed" (Prov 11:24–25).

"There were no needy persons among them. For from time to time those who owned lands or houses sold them, brought the money from the sales and put it at the apostles' feet, and it was distributed to anyone who had need" (Acts 4:34–35).

Model Compassion for Your Children

"Children's children are a crown to the aged, and parents are the pride of their children" (Prov 17:6).

"But if a widow has children or grandchildren, these should learn first of all to put their religion into practice by caring for their own family and so repaying their parents and grandparents, for this is pleasing to God" (1 Tim 5:4).

Give Money

"So when you give to the needy, do not announce it with trumpets, as the hypocrites do in the synagogues and on the streets, to be honored by others. Truly I tell you, they have received their reward in full. But when you give to the needy, do not let your left hand know what your right hand is doing, so that your giving may be in secret. Then your Father, who sees what is done in secret, will reward you" (Matt 6:2–4).

"Jesus sat down opposite the place where the offerings were put and watched the crowd putting their money into the temple treasury. Many rich people threw in large amounts. But a poor widow came and put in two very small copper coins, worth only a few cents. Calling his disciples to him, Jesus said, "Truly I tell you, this poor widow has put more into the treasury than all the others. They all gave out of their wealth; but she, out of her poverty, put in everything — all she had to live on" (Mark 12:41–44).

"Your prayers and gifts to the poor have come up as a memorial offering before God" (Acts 10:4b).

"After an absence of several years, I came to Jerusalem to bring my people gifts for the poor and to present offerings" (Acts 24:17).

"Now, however, I am on my way to Jerusalem in the service of the Lord's people there. For Macedonia and Achaia were pleased to make a contribution for the poor among the Lord's people in Jerusalem" (Rom 15:25 – 26).

"All they asked was that we should continue to remember the poor, the very thing I had been eager to do all along" (Gal 2:10).

"Remember this: Whoever sows sparingly will also reap sparingly, and whoever sows generously will also reap generously. Each of you should give what you have decided in your heart to give, not reluctantly or under compulsion, for God loves a cheerful giver. And God is able to bless you abundantly, so that in all things at all times, having all that you need, you will abound in every good work. As it is written: 'They have freely scattered their gifts to the poor; their righteousness endures forever.' Now he who supplies seed to the sower and bread for food will also supply and increase your store of seed and will enlarge the harvest of your righteousness. You will be enriched in every way so that you can be generous on every occasion, and through us your generosity will result in thanksgiving to God" (2 Cor 9:6 – 11).

Show Respect: A Lifestyle Choice

"My brothers and sisters, believers in our glorious Lord Jesus Christ must not show favoritism. Suppose a man comes into your meeting wearing a gold ring and fine clothes, and a poor man in filthy old clothes also comes in. If you show special attention to the man wearing fine clothes and say, 'Here's a good seat for you,' but say to the poor man, 'You stand there' or 'Sit on the floor by my feet,' have you not discriminated among yourselves and become judges with evil thoughts?

Listen, my dear brothers and sisters: Has not God chosen those who are poor in the eyes of the world to be rich in faith and to inherit the kingdom he promised those who love him? But you have dishonored the poor. Is it not the rich who are exploiting you? Are they not the ones who are dragging you into court? Are they not the ones who are blaspheming the noble name of him to whom you belong?

If you really keep the royal law found in Scripture, 'Love your neighbor as yourself,' you are doing right" (Jas 2:1 – 8).

Care for Spiritual Needs

"He raises the poor from the dust and lifts the needy from the ash heap; he seats them with princes and has them inherit a throne of honor" (1 Sam 2:8a).

"You gave abundant showers, O God; you refreshed your weary inheritance. Your people settled in it, and from your bounty, O God, you provided for the poor" (Ps 68:9 – 10).

"Better the poor whose walk is blameless than a fool whose lips are perverse" (Prov 19:1).

*　*　*

As you have worked your way through this list, perhaps other passages came to mind. Perhaps you noticed how many verses from the book of Proverbs were included — and because of this, we can safely conclude that Christian service is something that must be considered wise. In sum, though, such a list is intimidating. We could easily pour out the whole of our lives serving in any one of these areas (or other areas not included in this list). May God's Word in this way be a catalyst to spur us on to obedient action.

I'd like to choose just one example from the list above to help flesh out to a small degree how we might think about any of the possible paths of service in this list. Consider an item from this list that is less obvious and, on the surface, less intriguing. The idea that we as Christians might "fight for health care reform" might not strike you as a path for service that is closely tied to spreading the good news of the gospel of our Savior. But any of the paths of service listed here might similarly be disconnected from sharing the Word; this is a problem to be avoided at all costs. Bear in mind that many people who are not Christians have fed the poor or provided shelter to the homeless. Ensuring that all of our Christian service is closely connected to sharing the truth of Jesus with others must be understood as a constant in this equation.

As we have seen, Christians were among the first to build hospitals. This intelligent and efficient approach to caring for human beings in their physical extremity mirrors the great love God has shown to us. Would you want to live in a world where hospitals did not exist? Not all, however, have equal access to such care. So, for example, when Atul Gawande writes about how the medical system might be improved, he is not preaching the gospel (nor is he espousing Christian truth), but he makes sense as he explains how things might be improved in places such as India, China, and the United States.[2] We as Christians should be leading the way not only in driving positive and equitable change in such reform but also in connecting such actions with our love for Christ. I've heard it said that William Booth, the founder of the

Salvation Army, once reported, "Nobody gets a blessing if they have cold feet, and nobody ever got saved while they had a toothache!"

Much more could be said about this one issue of health care reform, which is the point. You should look at, review, and pray over this entire list. Allow God's Word to do its work. Pray about starting to serve in one or more areas, either on your own or as a part of your church. Indeed, urge your church to acts of service that are connected to the proclamation of the gospel. Which of these are you passionate about? Which of these could you see pouring your energy into? As you think about these things, you are taking the first steps toward loving your fellow human beings in a way that reveals your heartfelt love for God.

CONCLUSION

A DEAR FRIEND once shared her testimony with me about an early period in her Christian walk. You might find it a bit unsettling, as I did when she first shared it with me. Genuine testimonies of God's saving grace are sometimes messy, because they are real. My prayer in sharing hers here is that you will see how you yourself might be unwittingly affecting the lives of others either positively or negatively as you seek to serve the Lord. She writes,

> I got pregnant as a freshman in high school. I had sex just once for the first time and used protection. I found out I was pregnant a few months later. I was kicked off the basketball team, even though I had a doctor's note which would have allowed me to still play. My dreams faded slowly, but some of these things were not what God intended for my life. He had other plans, and brought a precious gift into my life, my daughter.
>
> I was brought up in a Christian home, and we went to church every Sunday and Wednesday. When everyone in church found out, I was the gossip on everyone's lips. I was called horrible names; it was as if I had become a virus. Most of my friends left me, because their parents thought I was a bad influence. All I had left was my family and the part of the church family that stood by me.
>
> I became very depressed and had to go to a doctor for help. If people had not treated me that way I would not have put myself down so much. I did stay in school while being a single mother, liv-

ing with my grandparents who provided for me. I graduated in the top ten of my class as a National Honor Society student. I proved to everyone in that small town that I could still be better than the other teen mothers that dropped out or were not there for their kids. As Christians we should look past the mistakes people make. We need to learn from them. God forgave me and that's all that counts. We should not judge teen mothers or fathers; instead, we should come alongside of them as Jesus Christ would.

I cannot see how our love for God can be disconnected from love for other human beings. In this precious, open, and honest account, we see how it is that God worked in this young woman's life, encouraging and strengthening her despite the hardheartedness of most of her fellow church members. I am hopeful that, like me, you are grateful that God was at work in the midst of this situation, bringing comfort and even blessing to her.

But rather than point a finger at those who knew my friend at this time, we should instead make an immediate personal application. As we look at the relationships we now have in our lives, can the people who know us see our love for God because we are loving toward them? Even more, are we aware that people are either drawn toward or away from loving God based on our actions? These are sobering questions.

In Matthew 9:13 and 12:7, Jesus looks back to Hosea 6:6 and emphasizes this crucial idea: "I desire mercy, not sacrifice." It may not be immediately obvious, but as we reflect on these few words, we must recognize that this is a stunning statement. We have perhaps been led to believe that, above all other things, the one thing that is most pleasing to God is our consistency in performing our religious ceremonies. In point of fact, though, our sacrifices — our worship, among other things — are utterly worthless if they are disconnected from a heart that beats not only with love for our God, but also with love for our fellow human beings (inside and outside the church). Over and over again, certainly in the famous 1 Corinthians 13 but also elsewhere, the apostle Paul talks about love as that characteristic of the Christian life that trumps all others. He writes:

> If I speak in the tongues of men or of angels, but do not have love, I am only a resounding gong or a clanging cymbal. If I have the gift of prophecy and can fathom all mysteries and all knowledge, and if I have a faith that can move mountains, but do not have love, I am nothing. If I give all I possess to the poor and give over my body to hardship that I may boast, but do not have love, I gain nothing. (1 Cor 13:1 – 3)

Similarly, in Micah 6:8, we read these famous words: "He has showed you, O mortal, what is good. And what does the LORD require of you? To act justly and to love mercy and to walk humbly with your God." Do you see here the intimate connection between a life of justice and mercy and of closeness to our God? This is "good," the prophet says.

Knowing how to live for God by loving him and others is potentially daunting, but at the same time, it's also a freeing thing. It's a heart of love. Wouldn't you agree? While there are hundreds of commandments and more than a thousand chapters in the Bible, Jesus drew our attention to just two. Will we love him with all of our heart, mind, soul, and strength? Will we love others? May the Lord bless you richly as you seek to do just this.

NOTES

Chapter 1: Love for God

1. A. B. Simpson, *The Self Life and the Christ Life* (Camp Hill, PA: Christian Publications, 1990), 19.

Chapter 2: Worship

1. A. W. Tozer, *The Knowledge of the Holy* (Harrisburg, PA: Christian Publications, 1961), 25.
2. A. W. Tozer, *Whatever Happened to Worship* (Camp Hill, PA: Christian Publications, 1985), 18–19.

Chapter 5: The Life of Prayer

1. This is taken from Pollock's hymn, "We Have Not Known Thee as We Ought."

Chapter 8: The Life of Service Leads to Opportunities for Evangelism and Missions

1. See Robert E. Coleman, *The Master Plan of Evangelism* (Grand Rapids: Baker, 2006).
2. See Rebecca M. Pippert, *Out of the Salt Shaker and into the World* (Downers Grove, IL: InterVarsity Press, 1999).
3. See www.campuscrusade.com/fourlawseng.htm (accessed January 26, 2012).
4. See D. James Kennedy, *Evangelism Explosion* (4th ed.; Wheaton, IL: Tyndale, 1996).

Chapter 9: Loving the Neighbors Near Our Homes

1. L. Shannon Jung, *Hunger and Happiness* (Minneapolis: Augsburg, 2009), 26.

Chapter 10: Loving Our Neighbor Elsewhere

1. See "Doing Missions When Dying Is Gain," at www.desiringgod.org/resource-library/conference-messages/doing-missions-when-dying-is-gain (accessed March 27, 2013).

Chapter 11: Areas of Possible Christian Service

1. Cathy Butler, *Breaking the Cycle: Issues Affecting Poverty* (Birmingham, AL: Women's Missionary Union, 2004), 11.
2. See Atul Gawande, *Better: A Surgeon's Notes on Performance* (New York: Metropolitan, 2007) or *The Checklist Manifesto: How to Get Things Right* (New York: Metropolitan, 2010).

Share Your Thoughts

With the Author: Your comments will be forwarded to the author when you send them to *zauthor@zondervan.com*.

With Zondervan: Submit your review of this book by writing to *zreview@zondervan.com*.

Free Online Resources at
www.zondervan.com

Daily Bible Verses and Devotions: Enrich your life with daily Bible verses or devotions that help you start every morning focused on God. Visit www.zondervan.com/newsletters.

Free Email Publications: Sign up for newsletters on Christian living, academic resources, church ministry, fiction, children's resources, and more. Visit www.zondervan.com/newsletters.

Zondervan Bible Search: Find and compare Bible passages in a variety of translations at www.zondervanbiblesearch.com.

Other Benefits: Register to receive online benefits like coupons and special offers, or to participate in research.